بِسْمِ اللهِ الرَّحْمَنِ الرَّحِيمِ

This ramadan journal belongs to:

My Weekly Planning.. 1

Monday
_____
_____
_____
_____

Tuesday
_____
_____
_____
_____

Wednesday
_____
_____
_____
_____

Thursday
_____
_____
_____
_____

Friday
_____
_____
_____
_____

Saturday
_____
_____
_____
_____

Sunday
_____
_____
_____
_____

Weekly Reflection
_____
_____
_____
_____

Bismillah

Fasting..

YES   NO

Prayer.. ✓

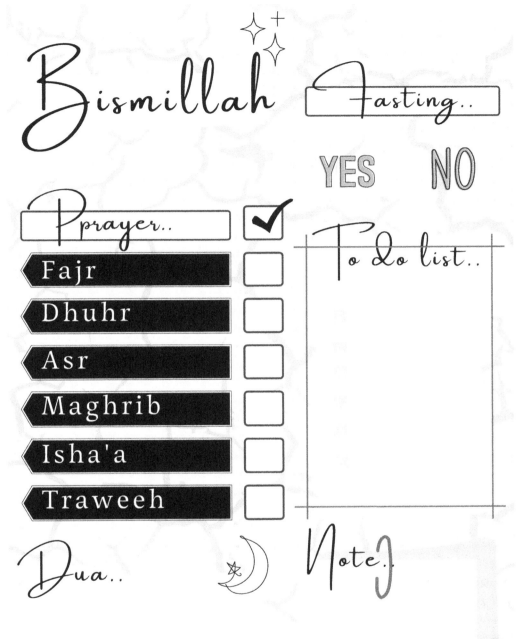

Fajr	☐
Dhuhr	☐
Asr	☐
Maghrib	☐
Isha'a	☐
Traweeh	☐

To do list..

Dua..

Note.

My Daily Planning..

TODAY I'M THANKFUL FOR ..

-
-
-
-
-

GOOD DEEDS..

MY THOUGHTS FOR THE DAY..

TODAY'S IFTAR..

TODAY'S SUHOOR..

QURAN READING..

- START/   SURAH: AYAH:

- FINISH/   SURAH: AYAH:

MY GOALS..

IMPORTANT..

- [ ] ....
- [ ] ....
- [ ] ....
- [ ] ....
- [ ] ....
- [ ] ....
- [ ] ....
- [ ] ....
- [ ] ....
- [ ] ....
- [ ] ....
- [ ] ....
- [ ] ....
- [ ] ....
....
....

My TO DO LIST

No.	To Do	Yes/No
....	....	....
....	....	....
....	....	....
....	....	....
....	....	....
....	....	....
....	....	....
....	....	....
....	....	....
....	....	....
....	....	....
....	....	....
....	....	....
....	....	....
....	....	....
....	....	....
....	....	....

Reminders for Today.. ....
....
....
....

Bismillah

Fasting..

YES   NO

Prayer.. ✔

Fajr ☐
Dhuhr ☐
Asr ☐
Maghrib ☐
Isha'a ☐
Traweeh ☐

To do list..

Dua..

Note.

My Daily Planning..

TODAY I'M THANKFUL FOR ..

-
-
-
-
-

GOOD DEEDS..

MY THOUGHTS FOR THE DAY..

TODAY'S IFTAR..

TODAY'S SUHOOR..

QURAN READING..

- START/   SURAH: AYAH:
- FINISH/   SURAH: AYAH:

MY GOALS..

IMPORTANT..

- ☐ ....
- ☐ ....
- ☐ ....
- ☐ ....
- ☐ ....
- ☐ ....
- ☐ ....
- ☐ ....
- ☐ ....
- ☐ ....
- ☐ ....
- ☐ ....
- ☐ ....
....
....

My TO DO LIST

No.	To Do	Yes/No
....	....	....
....	....	....
....	....	....
....	....	....
....	....	....
....	....	....
....	....	....
....	....	....
....	....	....
....	....	....
....	....	....
....	....	....
....	....	....
....	....	....
....	....	....
....	....	....
....	....	....
....	....	....
....	....	....

Reminders for Today..

Bismillah

Fasting..

YES   **NO**

Prayer.. ✔

- Fajr ☐
- Dhuhr ☐
- Asr ☐
- Maghrib ☐
- Isha'a ☐
- Traweeh ☐

To do list..

Dua..

Note.

My Daily Planning..

TODAY I'M THANKFUL FOR ..

-
-
-
-
-

GOOD DEEDS..

....
....
....
....
....

MY THOUGHTS FOR THE DAY..

....
....
....
....
....

TODAY'S IFTAR..

....
....
....
....
....

TODAY'S SUHOOR..

....
....
....
....
....

QURAN READING..

- START/   SURAH: AYAH:
- FINISH/   SURAH: AYAH:

MY GOALS..

....
....
....

IMPORTANT..

- [ ] ....
- [ ] ....
- [ ] ....
- [ ] ....
- [ ] ....
- [ ] ....
- [ ] ....
- [ ] ....
- [ ] ....
- [ ] ....
- [ ] ....
- [ ] ....
- [ ] ....
- [ ] ....

....

....

My TO DO LIST

No.	To Do	Yes/No
....	....	....
....	....	....
....	....	....
....	....	....
....	....	....
....	....	....
....	....	....
....	....	....
....	....	....
....	....	....
....	....	....
....	....	....
....	....	....
....	....	....
....	....	....
....	....	....
....	....	....
....	....	....

Reminders for Today..

....
....
....
....

Bismillah

Fasting..

YES　　NO

Prayer..	✔
Fajr	☐
Dhuhr	☐
Asr	☐
Maghrib	☐
Isha'a	☐
Traweeh	☐

To do list..

Dua..

Note:

My Daily Planning..

TODAY I'M THANKFUL FOR ..

-
-
-
-
-

GOOD DEEDS..

MY THOUGHTS FOR THE DAY..

TODAY'S IFTAR..

TODAY'S SUHOOR..

QURAN READING..

- START/   SURAH: AYAH:

- FINISH/   SURAH: AYAH:

MY GOALS..

IMPORTANT..

- [ ] ....
- [ ] ....
- [ ] ....
- [ ] ....
- [ ] ....
- [ ] ....
- [ ] ....
- [ ] ....
- [ ] ....
- [ ] ....
- [ ] ....
- [ ] ....
- [ ] ....
- [ ] ....

....

....

My TO DO LIST

No.	To Do	Yes/No
....	....	....
....	....	....
....	....	....
....	....	....
....	....	....
....	....	....
....	....	....
....	....	....
....	....	....
....	....	....
....	....	....
....	....	....
....	....	....
....	....	....
....	....	....
....	....	....
....	....	....
....	....	....

Reminders for Today..

Bismillah

Fasting..

YES   **NO**

Prayer.. ✓

- Fajr ☐
- Dhuhr ☐
- Asr ☐
- Maghrib ☐
- Isha'a ☐
- Traweeh ☐

To do list..

Dua..

Note..

My Daily Planning..

TODAY I'M THANKFUL FOR ..

-
-
-
-
-

GOOD DEEDS..

MY THOUGHTS FOR THE DAY..

TODAY'S IFTAR..

TODAY'S SUHOOR..

QURAN READING..

- START/ SURAH: AYAH:
- FINISH/ SURAH: AYAH:

MY GOALS..

IMPORTANT..

- [ ] ....
- [ ] ....
- [ ] ....
- [ ] ....
- [ ] ....
- [ ] ....
- [ ] ....
- [ ] ....
- [ ] ....
- [ ] ....
- [ ] ....
- [ ] ....
- [ ] ....
- [ ] ....

My TO DO LIST

No.	To Do	Yes/No
....	....	....
....	....	....
....	....	....
....	....	....
....	....	....
....	....	....
....	....	....
....	....	....
....	....	....
....	....	....
....	....	....
....	....	....
....	....	....
....	....	....
....	....	....
....	....	....
....	....	....
....	....	....

Reminders for Today..
....
....
....

Bismillah

Fasting..

YES   **NO**

Prayer.. ✔

- Fajr ☐
- Dhuhr ☐
- Asr ☐
- Maghrib ☐
- Isha'a ☐
- Traweeh ☐

To do list..

Dua..

Note..

My daily Planning..

TODAY I'M THANKFUL FOR ..

-
-
-
-
-

GOOD DEEDS..

....
....
....
....
....

MY THOUGHTS FOR THE DAY..

....
....
....
....
....

TODAY'S IFTAR..

....
....
....
....
....

TODAY'S SUHOOR..

....
....
....
....
....

QURAN READING..

- START/   SURAH: AYAH:

- FINISH/   SURAH: AYAH:

MY GOALS..

....
....
....

IMPORTANT..

- [ ] ....
- [ ] ....
- [ ] ....
- [ ] ....
- [ ] ....
- [ ] ....
- [ ] ....
- [ ] ....
- [ ] ....
- [ ] ....
- [ ] ....
- [ ] ....
- [ ] ....
....
....

My TO DO LIST

No.	To Do		Yes/No	
....	....		....	....
....	....		....	....
....	....		....	....
....	....		....	....
....	....		....	....
....	....		....	....
....	....		....	....
....	....		....	....
....	....		....	....
....	....		....	....
....	....		....	....
....	....		....	....
....	....		....	....
....	....		....	....
....	....		....	....
....	....		....	....
....	....		....	....
....	....		....	....
....	....		....	....

Reminders for Today..

Bismillah

Fasting..

YES   NO

Prayer..   ✓

- Fajr
- Dhuhr
- Asr
- Maghrib
- Isha'a
- Traweeh

To do list..

Dua..

Note..

My daily Planning..

TODAY I'M THANKFUL FOR ..

-
-
-
-
-

GOOD DEEDS..

....
....
....
....
....

MY THOUGHTS FOR THE DAY..

....
....
....
....
....

TODAY'S IFTAR..

....
....
....
....
....

TODAY'S SUHOOR..

....
....
....
....
....

QURAN READING..

- START/   SURAH: ....   AYAH: ....

- FINISH/   SURAH: ....   AYAH: ....

MY GOALS..

....
....
....

IMPORTANT..

- [ ] ....
- [ ] ....
- [ ] ....
- [ ] ....
- [ ] ....
- [ ] ....
- [ ] ....
- [ ] ....
- [ ] ....
- [ ] ....
- [ ] ....
- [ ] ....
- [ ] ....
- [ ] ....

My TO DO LIST

No.	To Do	Yes/No

Reminders for Today..

My Weekly Planning.. 2

Monday
_____
_____
_____
_____

Tuesday
_____
_____
_____
_____

Wednesday
_____
_____
_____

Thursday
_____
_____
_____

Friday
_____
_____
_____
_____

Saturday
_____
_____
_____
_____

Sunday
_____
_____
_____
_____

Weekly Reflection
_____
_____
_____
_____

Bismillah

Fasting..

YES   NO

Prayer.. ✓

- Fajr ☐
- Dhuhr ☐
- Asr ☐
- Maghrib ☐
- Isha'a ☐
- Traweeh ☐

To do list..

- ☐
- ☐
- ☐
- ☐
- ☐

Dua..

Note..

My daily Planning..

TODAY I'M THANKFUL FOR ..

-
-
-
-
-

GOOD DEEDS..

MY THOUGHTS FOR THE DAY..

TODAY'S IFTAR..

TODAY'S SUHOOR..

QURAN READING..

- START/   SURAH: AYAH:

- FINISH/   SURAH: AYAH:

MY GOALS..

IMPORTANT..

- [ ] ....
- [ ] ....
- [ ] ....
- [ ] ....
- [ ] ....
- [ ] ....
- [ ] ....
- [ ] ....
- [ ] ....
- [ ] ....
- [ ] ....
- [ ] ....
- [ ] ....
- [ ] ....
....
....

My TO DO LIST

No.	To Do	Yes/No
....	....	....
....	....	....
....	....	....
....	....	....
....	....	....
....	....	....
....	....	....
....	....	....
....	....	....
....	....	....
....	....	....
....	....	....
....	....	....
....	....	....
....	....	....
....	....	....
....	....	....
....	....	....

Reminders for Today..

Bismillah

Fasting..

YES   NO

Pprayer.. ✔

Fajr ☐

Dhuhr ☐

Asr ☐

Maghrib ☐

Isha'a ☐

Traweeh ☐

To do list..

Dua..

Note.

My daily Planning..

TODAY I'M THANKFUL FOR ..

-
-
-
-
-

GOOD DEEDS..

....

....

....

....

....

MY THOUGHTS FOR THE DAY..

....

....

....

....

....

TODAY'S IFTAR..

....

....

....

....

....

TODAY'S SUHOOR..

....

....

....

....

....

QURAN READING..

- START/ SURAH: _____ AYAH: _____

- FINISH/ SURAH: _____ AYAH: _____

MY GOALS..

....

....

....

IMPORTANT..

- ☐ ....
- ☐ ....
- ☐ ....
- ☐ ....
- ☐ ....
- ☐ ....
- ☐ ....
- ☐ ....
- ☐ ....
- ☐ ....
- ☐ ....
- ☐ ....
- ☐ ....
- ☐ ....

 **TO DO LIST**

No.	To Do	Yes/No
....	....	....
....	....	....
....	....	....
....	....	....
....	....	....
....	....	....
....	....	....
....	....	....
....	....	....
....	....	....
....	....	....
....	....	....
....	....	....
....	....	....
....	....	....
....	....	....
....	....	....
....	....	....
....	....	....
....	....	....

Reminders for Today.. ....

....

....

Bismillah

Fasting..

YES   **NO**

prayer.. ✔

- Fajr ☐
- Dhuhr ☐
- Asr ☐
- Maghrib ☐
- Isha'a ☐
- Traweeh ☐

To do list..

Dua..

Note.

My Daily Planning..

TODAY I'M THANKFUL FOR ..

-
-
-
-
-

GOOD DEEDS..

....

....

....

....

....

MY THOUGHTS FOR THE DAY..

....

....

....

....

....

TODAY'S IFTAR..

....

....

....

....

....

TODAY'S SUHOOR..

....

....

....

....

....

QURAN READING..

- START/   SURAH: ....   AYAH: ....

- FINISH/   SURAH: ....   AYAH: ....

MY GOALS..

....

....

....

IMPORTANT..

- [ ] ....
- [ ] ....
- [ ] ....
- [ ] ....
- [ ] ....
- [ ] ....
- [ ] ....
- [ ] ....
- [ ] ....
- [ ] ....
- [ ] ....
- [ ] ....
- [ ] ....
- [ ] ....
....
....

My TO DO LIST

No.	To Do	Yes/No
....	....	....
....	....	....
....	....	....
....	....	....
....	....	....
....	....	....
....	....	....
....	....	....
....	....	....
....	....	....
....	....	....
....	....	....
....	....	....
....	....	....
....	....	....
....	....	....
....	....	....
....	....	....
....	....	....
....	....	....

Reminders for Today..

Bismillah

Fasting..

YES   NO

Prayer..	✔
Fajr	☐
Dhuhr	☐
Asr	☐
Maghrib	☐
Isha'a	☐
Traweeh	☐

To do list..

Dua..

Note..

My daily Planning..

TODAY I'M THANKFUL FOR ..

-
-
-
-
-

GOOD DEEDS..

....
....
....
....
....

MY THOUGHTS FOR THE DAY..

....
....
....
....
....

TODAY'S IFTAR..

....
....
....
....
....

TODAY'S SUHOOR..

....
....
....
....
....

QURAN READING..

- START/   SURAH: AYAH:

- FINISH/   SURAH: AYAH:

MY GOALS..

....
....
....

IMPORTANT..

- [ ] ....
- [ ] ....
- [ ] ....
- [ ] ....
- [ ] ....
- [ ] ....
- [ ] ....
- [ ] ....
- [ ] ....
- [ ] ....
- [ ] ....
- [ ] ....
- [ ] ....
- [ ] ....

My TO DO LIST

No.	To Do	Yes/No
....	....	....
....	....	....
....	....	....
....	....	....
....	....	....
....	....	....
....	....	....
....	....	....
....	....	....
....	....	....
....	....	....
....	....	....
....	....	....
....	....	....
....	....	....
....	....	....
....	....	....
....	....	....
....	....	....

Reminders for Today..

Bismillah

Fasting..

YES   **NO**

Prayer.. ✓

- Fajr ☐
- Dhuhr ☐
- Asr ☐
- Maghrib ☐
- Isha'a ☐
- Traweeh ☐

To do list..

Dua..

Note.

My Daily Planning..

TODAY I'M THANKFUL FOR ..

-
-
-
-
-

GOOD DEEDS..

MY THOUGHTS FOR THE DAY..

TODAY'S IFTAR..

TODAY'S SUHOOR..

QURAN READING..

- START/   SURAH: AYAH:

- FINISH/   SURAH: AYAH:

MY GOALS..

IMPORTANT..

- [ ] ....
- [ ] ....
- [ ] ....
- [ ] ....
- [ ] ....
- [ ] ....
- [ ] ....
- [ ] ....
- [ ] ....
- [ ] ....
- [ ] ....
- [ ] ....
- [ ] ....
- [ ] ....

My TO DO LIST

No.	To Do	Yes/No	
....	....	....	....
....	....	....	....
....	....	....	....
....	....	....	....
....	....	....	....
....	....	....	....
....	....	....	....
....	....	....	....
....	....	....	....
....	....	....	....
....	....	....	....
....	....	....	....
....	....	....	....
....	....	....	....
....	....	....	....
....	....	....	....
....	....	....	....
....	....	....	....
....	....	....	....

Reminders for Today..
....
....
....

Bismillah

Fasting..

YES   NO

Prayer.. ☑

Fajr ☐
Dhuhr ☐
Asr ☐
Maghrib ☐
Isha'a ☐
Traweeh ☐

To do list..

Dua..

Note.

My Daily Planning..

TODAY I'M THANKFUL FOR ..

-
-
-
-
-

GOOD DEEDS..

MY THOUGHTS FOR THE DAY..

TODAY'S IFTAR..

TODAY'S SUHOOR..

QURAN READING..

- START/   SURAH: AYAH:

- FINISH/   SURAH: AYAH:

MY GOALS..

IMPORTANT..

- ☐ ....
- ☐ ....
- ☐ ....
- ☐ ....
- ☐ ....
- ☐ ....
- ☐ ....
- ☐ ....
- ☐ ....
- ☐ ....
- ☐ ....
- ☐ ....
- ☐ ....
- ☐ ....

My TO DO LIST

No.	To Do	Yes/No
....	....	....
....	....	....
....	....	....
....	....	....
....	....	....
....	....	....
....	....	....
....	....	....
....	....	....
....	....	....
....	....	....
....	....	....
....	....	....
....	....	....
....	....	....
....	....	....
....	....	....
....	....	....
....	....	....
....	....	....
....	....	....

Reminders for Today.. ....
....
....
....

Bismillah

Fasting..

YES   **NO**

Prayer.. ✓

- Fajr ☐
- Dhuhr ☐
- Asr ☐
- Maghrib ☐
- Isha'a ☐
- Traweeh ☐

To do list..

Dua..

Note.

My daily Planning..

TODAY I'M THANKFUL FOR ..

-
-
-
-
-

GOOD DEEDS..

....
....
....
....
....

MY THOUGHTS FOR THE DAY..

....
....
....
....
....

TODAY'S IFTAR..

....
....
....
....
....

TODAY'S SUHOOR..

....
....
....
....
....

QURAN READING..

- START/   SURAH: ....   AYAH: ....

- FINISH/   SURAH: ....   AYAH: ....

MY GOALS..

....
....
....

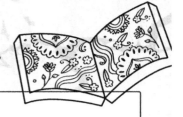

IMPORTANT..

- [ ] ....
- [ ] ....
- [ ] ....
- [ ] ....
- [ ] ....
- [ ] ....
- [ ] ....
- [ ] ....
- [ ] ....
- [ ] ....
- [ ] ....
- [ ] ....
- [ ] ....
- [ ] ....

....
....

My TO DO LIST

No.	To Do	Yes/No	
....	....	....	....
....	....	....	....
....	....	....	....
....	....	....	....
....	....	....	....
....	....	....	....
....	....	....	....
....	....	....	....
....	....	....	....
....	....	....	....
....	....	....	....
....	....	....	....
....	....	....	....
....	....	....	....
....	....	....	....
....	....	....	....
....	....	....	....
....	....	....	....

Reminders for Today..

My Weekly Planning...3

Monday

_____
_____
_____
_____

Tuesday

_____
_____
_____
_____

Wednesday

_____
_____
_____
_____

Thursday

_____
_____
_____
_____

Friday

_____
_____
_____
_____

Saturday

_____
_____
_____
_____

Sunday

_____
_____
_____
_____

Weekly Reflection

_____
_____
_____
_____

Bismillah

Fasting..

YES   NO

Prayer.. ✓

- Fajr
- Dhuhr
- Asr
- Maghrib
- Isha'a
- Traweeh

To do list..

Dua..

Note.

My Daily Planning..

TODAY I'M THANKFUL FOR ..

-
-
-
-
-

GOOD DEEDS..

MY THOUGHTS FOR THE DAY..

TODAY'S IFTAR..

TODAY'S SUHOOR..

QURAN READING..

- START/   SURAH: AYAH:

- FINISH/   SURAH: AYAH:

MY GOALS..

IMPORTANT..

- ☐ ....
- ☐ ....
- ☐ ....
- ☐ ....
- ☐ ....
- ☐ ....
- ☐ ....
- ☐ ....
- ☐ ....
- ☐ ....
- ☐ ....
- ☐ ....
- ☐ ....

....

....

My TO DO LIST

No.	To Do	Yes/No
....	....	....
....	....	....
....	....	....
....	....	....
....	....	....
....	....	....
....	....	....
....	....	....
....	....	....
....	....	....
....	....	....
....	....	....
....	....	....
....	....	....
....	....	....
....	....	....
....	....	....
....	....	....

Reminders for Today..
....
....
....

Bismillah

Fasting..

YES   NO

Prayer.. ✔

- Fajr
- Dhuhr
- Asr
- Maghrib
- Isha'a
- Traweeh

To do list..

Dua..

Note.

My daily Planning..

TODAY I'M THANKFUL FOR ..

-
-
-
-
-

GOOD DEEDS..

MY THOUGHTS FOR THE DAY..

TODAY'S IFTAR..

TODAY'S SUHOOR..

QURAN READING..

- START/   SURAH: AYAH:

- FINISH/ SURAH: AYAH:

MY GOALS..

IMPORTANT..

- [ ] ....
- [ ] ....
- [ ] ....
- [ ] ....
- [ ] ....
- [ ] ....
- [ ] ....
- [ ] ....
- [ ] ....
- [ ] ....
- [ ] ....
- [ ] ....
- [ ] ....
....
....

My TO DO LIST

No.	To Do	Yes/No

Reminders for Today..

Bismillah

Fasting..

YES   **NO**

Prayer.. ✓

- Fajr ☐
- Dhuhr ☐
- Asr ☐
- Maghrib ☐
- Isha'a ☐
- Traweeh ☐

To do list..

Dua..

Note..

My daily Planning..

TODAY I'M THANKFUL FOR ..

-
-
-
-
-

GOOD DEEDS..

....
....
....
....
....

MY THOUGHTS FOR THE DAY..

....
....
....
....
....

TODAY'S IFTAR..

....
....
....
....
....

TODAY'S SUHOOR..

....
....
....
....
....

QURAN READING..

- START/   SURAH: AYAH:

- FINISH/ SURAH: AYAH:

MY GOALS..

....
....
....

IMPORTANT..

- [ ] ....
- [ ] ....
- [ ] ....
- [ ] ....
- [ ] ....
- [ ] ....
- [ ] ....
- [ ] ....
- [ ] ....
- [ ] ....
- [ ] ....
- [ ] ....
- [ ] ....

My TO DO LIST

No.	To Do	Yes/No
....	....	....
....	....	....
....	....	....
....	....	....
....	....	....
....	....	....
....	....	....
....	....	....
....	....	....
....	....	....
....	....	....
....	....	....
....	....	....
....	....	....
....	....	....
....	....	....
....	....	....
....	....	....

Reminders for Today..

Bismillah

Fasting..

YES   **NO**

Prayer.. ✓

- Fajr ☐
- Dhuhr ☐
- Asr ☐
- Maghrib ☐
- Isha'a ☐
- Traweeh ☐

To do list..

Dua..

Note.

My Daily Planning..

TODAY I'M THANKFUL FOR ..

-
-
-
-
-

GOOD DEEDS..

....
....
....
....
....

MY THOUGHTS FOR THE DAY..

....
....
....
....
....

TODAY'S IFTAR..

....
....
....
....
....

TODAY'S SUHOOR..

....
....
....
....
....

QURAN READING..

- START/   SURAH: ....   AYAH: ....

- FINISH/   SURAH: ....   AYAH: ....

MY GOALS..

....
....
....

IMPORTANT..

- [ ] ....
- [ ] ....
- [ ] ....
- [ ] ....
- [ ] ....
- [ ] ....
- [ ] ....
- [ ] ....
- [ ] ....
- [ ] ....
- [ ] ....
- [ ] ....
- [ ] ....

....

....

My TO DO LIST

No.	To Do	Yes/No
....	....	....
....	....	....
....	....	....
....	....	....
....	....	....
....	....	....
....	....	....
....	....	....
....	....	....
....	....	....
....	....	....
....	....	....
....	....	....
....	....	....
....	....	....
....	....	....
....	....	....
....	....	....
....	....	....
....	....	....

Reminders for Today..

Bismillah

Fasting..

YES   **NO**

Prayer.. ✔

- Fajr ☐
- Dhuhr ☐
- Asr ☐
- Maghrib ☐
- Isha'a ☐
- Traweeh ☐

To do list..

Dua..

Note.

My Daily Planning..

TODAY I'M THANKFUL FOR ..

-
-
-
-
-

GOOD DEEDS..

....
....
....
....
....

MY THOUGHTS FOR THE DAY..

....
....
....
....
....

TODAY'S IFTAR..

....
....
....
....
....

TODAY'S SUHOOR..

....
....
....
....
....

QURAN READING..

- START/   SURAH: AYAH:
- FINISH/   SURAH: AYAH:

MY GOALS..

....
....
....

IMPORTANT..

- [ ] ....
- [ ] ....
- [ ] ....
- [ ] ....
- [ ] ....
- [ ] ....
- [ ] ....
- [ ] ....
- [ ] ....
- [ ] ....
- [ ] ....
- [ ] ....
- [ ] ....
- [ ] ....

My TO DO LIST

No.	To Do	Yes/No	
....	....	....	....
....	....	....	....
....	....	....	....
....	....	....	....
....	....	....	....
....	....	....	....
....	....	....	....
....	....	....	....
....	....	....	....
....	....	....	....
....	....	....	....
....	....	....	....
....	....	....	....
....	....	....	....
....	....	....	....
....	....	....	....
....	....	....	....
....	....	....	....

Reminders for Today..

Bismillah

Fasting..

YES   NO

Pprayer..   ✔

Prayer	
Fajr	☐
Dhuhr	☐
Asr	☐
Maghrib	☐
Isha'a	☐
Traweeh	☐

To do list..

Dua..

Note.

My Daily Planning..

TODAY I'M THANKFUL FOR ..

-
-
-
-
-

GOOD DEEDS..

MY THOUGHTS FOR THE DAY..

TODAY'S IFTAR..

TODAY'S SUHOOR..

QURAN READING..

- START/   SURAH: AYAH:

- FINISH/   SURAH: AYAH:

MY GOALS..

IMPORTANT..

- [ ] ....
- [ ] ....
- [ ] ....
- [ ] ....
- [ ] ....
- [ ] ....
- [ ] ....
- [ ] ....
- [ ] ....
- [ ] ....
- [ ] ....
- [ ] ....
- [ ] ....
- [ ] ....
....
....

My TO DO LIST

No.	To Do	Yes/No

Reminders for Today..

Bismillah

Fasting..

YES **NO**

Prayer.. ☑

- Fajr ☐
- Dhuhr ☐
- Asr ☐
- Maghrib ☐
- Isha'a ☐
- Traweeh ☐

To do list..

Dua..

Note.

My Daily Planning..

TODAY I'M THANKFUL FOR ..

-
-
-
-
-

GOOD DEEDS..

....
....
....
....
....

MY THOUGHTS FOR THE DAY..

....
....
....
....
....

TODAY'S IFTAR..

....
....
....
....
....

TODAY'S SUHOOR..

....
....
....
....
....

QURAN READING..

- START/   SURAH: ....   AYAH: ....

- FINISH/   SURAH: ....   AYAH: ....

MY GOALS..

....
....
....

IMPORTANT..

- [ ] ....
- [ ] ....
- [ ] ....
- [ ] ....
- [ ] ....
- [ ] ....
- [ ] ....
- [ ] ....
- [ ] ....
- [ ] ....
- [ ] ....
- [ ] ....
- [ ] ....

....

....

My TO DO LIST

No.	To Do	Yes/No

Reminders for Today..

My Weekly Planning..4

Monday

_____
_____
_____
_____

Tuesday

_____
_____
_____
_____

Wednesday

_____
_____
_____
_____

Thursday

_____
_____
_____
_____

Friday

_____
_____
_____
_____

Saturday

_____
_____
_____
_____

Sunday

_____
_____
_____
_____

Weekly Reflection

_____
_____
_____
_____

Bismillah

Fasting..

YES   **NO**

Prayer.. ✓

- Fajr ☐
- Dhuhr ☐
- Asr ☐
- Maghrib ☐
- Isha'a ☐
- Traweeh ☐

To do list..

Dua..

Note.

My Daily Planning..

TODAY I'M THANKFUL FOR ..

-
-
-
-
-

GOOD DEEDS..

MY THOUGHTS FOR THE DAY..

TODAY'S IFTAR..

TODAY'S SUHOOR..

QURAN READING..

- START/   SURAH: AYAH:

- FINISH/   SURAH: AYAH:

MY GOALS..

IMPORTANT..

- [ ] ....
- [ ] ....
- [ ] ....
- [ ] ....
- [ ] ....
- [ ] ....
- [ ] ....
- [ ] ....
- [ ] ....
- [ ] ....
- [ ] ....
- [ ] ....
- [ ] ....
- [ ] ....
....
....

My TO DO LIST

No.	To Do	Yes/No
....	....	....
....	....	....
....	....	....
....	....	....
....	....	....
....	....	....
....	....	....
....	....	....
....	....	....
....	....	....
....	....	....
....	....	....
....	....	....
....	....	....
....	....	....
....	....	....
....	....	....
....	....	....
....	....	....

Reminders for Today..
....
....
....

Bismillah

Fasting..

YES   **NO**

Prayer.. ✔

- Fajr ☐
- Dhuhr ☐
- Asr ☐
- Maghrib ☐
- Isha'a ☐
- Traweeh ☐

To do list..

Dua..

Note.

My Daily Planning..

TODAY I'M THANKFUL FOR ..

-
-
-
-
-

GOOD DEEDS..

....
....
....
....
....

MY THOUGHTS FOR THE DAY..

....
....
....
....
....

TODAY'S IFTAR..

....
....
....
....
....

TODAY'S SUHOOR..

....
....
....
....
....

QURAN READING..

- START/   SURAH: ....   AYAH: ....

- FINISH/   SURAH: ....   AYAH: ....

MY GOALS..

....
....
....

IMPORTANT..

- ☐ ....
- ☐ ....
- ☐ ....
- ☐ ....
- ☐ ....
- ☐ ....
- ☐ ....
- ☐ ....
- ☐ ....
- ☐ ....
- ☐ ....
- ☐ ....
- ☐ ....
- ☐ ....

....

My TO DO LIST

No.	To Do	Yes/No	
....	....	....	....
....	....	....	....
....	....	....	....
....	....	....	....
....	....	....	....
....	....	....	....
....	....	....	....
....	....	....	....
....	....	....	....
....	....	....	....
....	....	....	....
....	....	....	....
....	....	....	....
....	....	....	....
....	....	....	....
....	....	....	....
....	....	....	....
....	....	....	....
....	....	....	....

Reminders for Today.. ....
....
....

Bismillah

Fasting..

YES   NO

Prayer.. ✓

- Fajr
- Dhuhr
- Asr
- Maghrib
- Isha'a
- Traweeh

To do list..

Dua..

Note..

My Daily Planning..

TODAY I'M THANKFUL FOR ..

-
-
-
-
-

GOOD DEEDS..

MY THOUGHTS FOR THE DAY..

TODAY'S IFTAR..

TODAY'S SUHOOR..

QURAN READING..

- START/   SURAH: AYAH:

- FINISH/   SURAH: AYAH:

MY GOALS..

IMPORTANT..

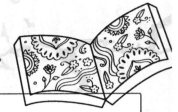

- [ ] ....
- [ ] ....
- [ ] ....
- [ ] ....
- [ ] ....
- [ ] ....
- [ ] ....
- [ ] ....
- [ ] ....
- [ ] ....
- [ ] ....
- [ ] ....
- [ ] ....
- [ ] ....
....
....

My TO DO LIST

No.	To Do	Yes/No

Reminders for Today..

Bismillah

Fasting..

YES   NO

Prayer..   ✔

Fajr

Dhuhr

Asr

Maghrib

Isha'a

Traweeh

To do list..

Dua..

Note..

My Daily Planning..

TODAY I'M THANKFUL FOR ..

-
-
-
-
-

GOOD DEEDS..

MY THOUGHTS FOR THE DAY..

TODAY'S IFTAR..

TODAY'S SUHOOR..

QURAN READING..

- START/   SURAH: AYAH:

- FINISH/   SURAH: AYAH:

MY GOALS..

IMPORTANT..

- [ ] ....
- [ ] ....
- [ ] ....
- [ ] ....
- [ ] ....
- [ ] ....
- [ ] ....
- [ ] ....
- [ ] ....
- [ ] ....
- [ ] ....
- [ ] ....
- [ ] ....
- [ ] ....

....

....

My TO DO LIST

No.	To Do	Yes/No
....	....	....
....	....	....
....	....	....
....	....	....
....	....	....
....	....	....
....	....	....
....	....	....
....	....	....
....	....	....
....	....	....
....	....	....
....	....	....
....	....	....
....	....	....
....	....	....
....	....	....
....	....	....
....	....	....

Reminders for Today..

Bismillah

Fasting..

YES   NO

Prayer..   ✔

Fajr   ☐
Dhuhr   ☐
Asr   ☐
Maghrib   ☐
Isha'a   ☐
Traweeh   ☐

To do list..

Dua..

Note..

My daily Planning..

TODAY I'M THANKFUL FOR ..

-
-
-
-
-

GOOD DEEDS..

MY THOUGHTS FOR THE DAY..

TODAY'S IFTAR..

TODAY'S SUHOOR..

QURAN READING..

- START/   SURAH: AYAH:

- FINISH/   SURAH: AYAH:

MY GOALS..

IMPORTANT..

- [ ] ....
- [ ] ....
- [ ] ....
- [ ] ....
- [ ] ....
- [ ] ....
- [ ] ....
- [ ] ....
- [ ] ....
- [ ] ....
- [ ] ....
- [ ] ....
- [ ] ....
....
....

My TO DO LIST

No.	To Do	Yes/No

Reminders for Today..

Bismillah

Fasting..

YES   NO

Prayer.. ✔

Fajr ☐

Dhuhr ☐

Asr ☐

Maghrib ☐

Isha'a ☐

Traweeh ☐

To do list..

Dua..

Note..

My Daily Planning..

TODAY I'M THANKFUL FOR ..

-
-
-
-
-

GOOD DEEDS..

MY THOUGHTS FOR THE DAY..

TODAY'S IFTAR..

TODAY'S SUHOOR..

QURAN READING..

- START/   SURAH: AYAH:
- FINISH/   SURAH: AYAH:

MY GOALS..

IMPORTANT..

- [ ] ....
- [ ] ....
- [ ] ....
- [ ] ....
- [ ] ....
- [ ] ....
- [ ] ....
- [ ] ....
- [ ] ....
- [ ] ....
- [ ] ....
- [ ] ....
- [ ] ....
- [ ] ....
....
....

My TO DO LIST

No.	To Do	Yes/No
....	....	....
....	....	....
....	....	....
....	....	....
....	....	....
....	....	....
....	....	....
....	....	....
....	....	....
....	....	....
....	....	....
....	....	....
....	....	....
....	....	....
....	....	....
....	....	....

Reminders for Today.. ....

....

....

Bismillah

Fasting..

YES   NO

Prayer.. ✔

Fajr	☐
Dhuhr	☐
Asr	☐
Maghrib	☐
Isha'a	☐
Traweeh	☐

To do list..

Dua..

Note..

My daily Planning..

TODAY I'M THANKFUL FOR ..

-
-
-
-
-

GOOD DEEDS..

MY THOUGHTS FOR THE DAY..

TODAY'S IFTAR..

TODAY'S SUHOOR..

QURAN READING..

- START/ SURAH: AYAH:

- FINISH/ SURAH: AYAH:

MY GOALS..

IMPORTANT..

- [ ] ....
- [ ] ....
- [ ] ....
- [ ] ....
- [ ] ....
- [ ] ....
- [ ] ....
- [ ] ....
- [ ] ....
- [ ] ....
- [ ] ....
- [ ] ....
- [ ] ....
- [ ] ....

My TO DO LIST

No.	To Do	Yes/No
....	....	....
....	....	....
....	....	....
....	....	....
....	....	....
....	....	....
....	....	....
....	....	....
....	....	....
....	....	....
....	....	....
....	....	....
....	....	....
....	....	....
....	....	....
....	....	....
....	....	....
....	....	....

Reminders for Today..

the last 2 days of ramadan

PLAN AND IDEAS TO FINISH MY RAMADAN

READY FOR EID..

- --
- --
- --
- --
- --
- --
- --

PRIORITY:

IDEAS TO PUT A SPECIAL END..

----

my best ramadan

dua for everything i love

myself _____

_____

_____

_____

_____

_____

_____

_____

my family _____

_____

_____

_____

_____

_____

_____

my friends _____

_____

_____

_____

_____

_____

_____

Goals for last day of ramadan

_____

_____

_____

_____

_____

the last iftar

_____

_____

_____

the last suhoor

_____

_____

_____

i'm thankful for

_____

_____

Notes

_____

_____

_____

_____

_____

_____

_____

_____

a word for this ramadan and goals for the next ramadan

_____

_____

_____

_____

_____

_____

_____

_____

_____

_____

_____

_____

Made in the USA
Las Vegas, NV
15 March 2022

45672246R00069